Also by Stephen Oliver

Henwise (1975)
& interviews (1978)
Autumn Songs (1978)
Letter To James K. Baxter (1980)
Earthbound Mirrors (1984)
Guardians, Not Angels (1993)
Islands of Wilderness—A Romance (1996)
Unmanned (1999)
Election Year Blues (1999)
Night of Warehouses: Poems 1978–2000 (2001)
Deadly Pollen (2003)
Ballads, Satire & Salt—A Book of Diversions (2003)
Either Side The Horizon (2005)
Parable Of The Sea Sponge (2007)
Harmonic (2008)
Apocrypha (2010)
Intercolonial (2013)
Gone: Satirical Poems: New & Selected (2016)

Recordings

Earthbound Mirrors, a selection, Stephen Oliver,
Ode Records (audio cassette) Auckland, Aotearoa / New Zealand, 1984

KING HIT: CD ROM. Stephen Oliver reads a selection of his poetry to original music composed by Matt Ottley. Published and released through IP Digital, an imprint of IP (Interactive Publications) Brisbane, Australia, 2007

LUXEMBOURG

POEMS BY

STEPHEN OLIVER

GP
GREYWACKE PRESS
Lat. 25°/50° South. Long. 145°/180° East

First Published 2018

Greywacke Press
9 Lynch St
Hughes
ACT 2605
Australia
reid1801@bigpond.com
greywackepress@gmail.com

Oliver, Stephen, 1950-
Title: *Luxembourg*
ISBN   978-0-646-98696-8

Cover design: Stephen Oliver
Cover photo: Jossy Gerö by Barbara Leytus née Neustädtl at Vegagasse, Vienna

A catalogue record for this book is available from the National Library of Australia

© Stephen Oliver

All rights reserved.
No part of this publication may be reproduced, stored in a retrieval system, or transmitted in any form or by any means, electronic, mechanical, photocopying, scanning, recording or otherwise, without the prior permission of the copyright owner.

Acknowledgements

Various poems first appeared in these print/online publications some in a variant form:

Antipodes, A Global Journal of Australian/New Zealand Literature (USA/Australia); *Asian Journal of Literature, Culture and Society* (Assumption University of Thailand, Bangkok); *Beattie's Book Blog* (NZ); *Beton* (Serbia); *Big Bridge* (USA); *Broadsheet Nos: 1/6, featured poet No.16* (NZ); *Cardinal Points Literary Journal: Vol. 6* (New York); *Contrappasso* (Australia); *Cordite Poetry Review 52: TRANSTASMAN issue* (Australia); *Eye To The Telescope* (USA); *Eureka Street* (Australia); *49 Writers* (Alaska); *InDaily* (Adelaide); *Landfall* (NZ); *London Grip* (UK); *Manifesto: An Anthology of 101 Political Poems*, edited by Emma Neale and Philip Temple, OUP, (2017); *Morning Star* (UK); *Plumwood Mountain* (Australia); *The Innisfree Poetry Journal* (Ireland); *Poetry NZ Yearbook 2*; *The Prose Poem Project* (USA); *Red Room Company, 'The Disappearing'* (Australia); *European Space Agency* (ESA); *Snorkel* (Australia); *Southerly* (Australia); *Spintongues* (Russia); *Starch* (NZ); *The Age of Translation Anthology*, Selected by Eugen V. Witkowsky (Russia); *Translit* (Russia); *3Quarks Daily* (USA); *Verity La* (Australia); *Wet Ink* (Australia).

Vek Pevoda / The Age of Translation is an evolving website anthology founded in 2003 by the famous Russian writer and translator, Eugen V. Witkowsky. Several anthologies have been published based upon this resource by Vodolei Publishers (Moscow) and more are planned.

My thanks to Dr. Heinz Leonhard (Leo) Kretzenbacher, German Studies, School of Languages and Linguistics, the University of Melbourne, who translated into German the title poem 'Luxembourg'.

'Open-Learning Workshops' belongs to the 'Chart Satire' genre— see: the Notes to *New Year Letter* by W.H. Auden, Faber & Faber 1941, and *Enemies of Promise* by Cyril Connolly, Penguin 1961.

A number of these poems first published as a chapbook titled, *Apocrypha*, Cold Hub Press (2010); 'The Great Repression' and 'This Way Out' first released as street poster poems by Phantom Billstickers (2010–11).

'The *Wow! Signal*' was a strong radio signal detected by Dr Jerry R. Ehman on August 15, 1977 while working on a SETI Project at The Big Ear radio telescope of Ohio State University.

My thanks to the Moscow-based translator/editor, Max Nemtsov, originally from Vladivostok, who translated into Russian the poem 'Streets of Kiev' published in *Beton; Cardinal Points Literary Journal; The Age of Translation Anthology; Manifesto: An Anthology of 101 Political Poems; Red Room Company; Spintongues; Translit; 3Quarks Daily*.

'Streets of Kiev' was read on my behalf by George Szirtes, the Hungarian-born poet and translator, as part of the 'Writing Human Rights' series of events organized by the University of East Anglia in Norwich, November 2015.

'The Great Rogatus' published on YouTube as a video poem, produced and read by the author, September (2014); 'Streets of Kiev' published on YouTube as a video poem, produced by the author and read in Russian by Max Nemtsov, June (2015); 'Still Breathing' published on YouTube as a video poem, produced and read by the author, August (2017).

'Jacob's Ladder' published on the ESA (European Space Agency) sponsored platform *Rosetta Art Tribute* along with a recording of the poem by the author.

I am most grateful to Nicole Sprague, spouse of Derick Burleson, and mother of their daughter Mirabel, who read my elegy 'Still Breathing' at his memorial, April 2017 in Fairbanks, Alaska. I never met Derick in person but we established a friendship via correspondence. He died aged fifty-three December 2016 in Fairbanks of an undiagnosed illness.

Contents

Dreams of Flying 3
El Niño 4
The Map 5
The Last Day Before 7
Electrician 8
Anthropolite Man 9
The Great Repression 10
Undercover 11
Another *Wow! Signal* 13
'No Pen or Paper in Paradise' 14
Millefiori 15
A Midwinter Night's Dream 16
Green Asterisk 17
Tracking Rupert Brooke 19
Apocrypha 20
Camber Swing 21
The Departed Guest 22
Scarecrow 23
Road Notes 24
Sister To The Sphinx 30
This Way Out 31
Titan Love Song 32
Baked Potato 34
The Transformation 35
Testament 36
Lace 37
Rendezvous 39
Nocturne 40
House of Occlusion 41
The Three Pillars 42
Rising Ghostly 44

Dark Matter 45
Domes 46
Choristers 47
The Waiting 48
Phalanxes 49
Stone Urns 50
Amongst Vine Leaves 52
Written In The Margins 53
Broken 54
Yellow Chevrons 55
The Vendors 56
Comb 57
Still Life With Boulders 58
The World's Basement 59
What Angels Throw 60
Breaking Straws 61
Stone Lintel 62
Dilapidated Dream 63
Duende 64
Cockaigne 65
The Great Rogatus 66
Slow Release 67
Luxembourg 68
In The Blink 70
Worry Beads 71
Signs 72
Open-Learning Workshops 73
   morning
   afternoon
   evening
Kitchen Table 79
At The Turn 80
The Lost German Girl 81
Dissentient 83

Streets of Kiev 87
Building Code 88
Silent As A Lantern 89
Impress 91
Black Swans 92
Jacob's Ladder 93
The Journey 94
Still Breathing 95

LUXEMBOURG

DREAMS OF FLYING

A building of red brick,
(once The Institute For The Blind);
an up-market café.
Desiccated, middle-aged matriarchs
come to water here,
where once the blind sat in the
open courtyard to take the early sun.
The women, it is observed,
refuse eye contact, stitched up,
moneyed and mummified, hold onto an
invisible safety rope that guides
them from car to counter.

The stillness of their panic
and paranoia is palpable, though they
are blind to that, too. On the
first floor balcony over the doorway,
a man hangs out two oriental
mats in the morning sun.
Dust motes mingle in the slipstream
of the hurrying blondes.
They are unravelling, winding sheets
of dry, sexual longing as they
complete the morning's checklist;
dreaming, perhaps, beneath
hanging oriental mats, of flying
into the arms of the languid waiter.

EL NIÑO

An argent sunset. And you know it is autumn
in Te Kuiti; a swift's wing chips light into the barn.

You give, much as you reject; ancient vision
turning on a land grab. Telegraph lines cast skid

marks loopingly all along this backcountry road.
Pine plantations hedgehog hills out of town.

A still paddock. Wind painted poplars. Leaves
rattle, breathe out, 'Devil's in the detail,' they say,

'from this questioning shore, to that fatal one,
yarns away.' My thumbnail brushes a fingerprint,

and the coin spins into the deep. A valve, aflutter.
Hollow rasping from the throat of the giant elm.

THE MAP

Atrocious snow blanketed the village.
Only the rounded portals of yellow
light indicated where windows had been.
One skeletal church spire rose above
the laden rooftops. Alpine valleys blurred
under plush darkness, the fossilized,
soft contours of this night-bound place.
In the market square, the *clerici vagantes*
declared that ego had collapsed under
its own weight, subsided into the sinkhole
of self-adulation; poets were complicit,
they said, the mind finally turned wolf
and consumed its young, language bowed
before an absurdist code of linguistics.

Twilight of the Anthropocene Age:
we soon deluded ourselves in the belief
that panic did not exist by pursuing
rational exegesis, systematic amassing of
information superseded the biomass.
A false sense of security prevailed
in cities that promised little beyond what
was known, the tuneless instruments
of lyricists now cast aside, administration
blocks amplified the hollow breath
of air conditioning—clack of keyboards.
Barbarism grew rank in desert regions,
mountain fastnesses, across borderlands;
raw recruits convened as death cults.
Terror and tribalism, enmeshed in mortal

combat, waged war against pluralism
and the present for a mediaeval caliphate
that never existed, as if time played
itself back somehow, and paradise shone
retrospectively.

                Time stretched
like tendons of an overworked athlete.
'Was memory a dangerous place?'
He marked it out on the map, got as far
as the snow line, and there he rested,
cigarette aglow, staring into the distance.
Cold played upon him, in the way that
a harmonica recalls pond-stillness.
He died where he squatted, eyes held the
same fixed stare that he had in life,
pupils dilated as the sun contracted west,
his face, momentarily, a golden mask.

THE LAST DAY BEFORE

The painter has not arrived yet.
Clouds slant back from hills, toward,
and untoward; no, he will not
come, given his gaze is held otherwise,
a scene gaudy, maybe, to his inner-eye.

Though brush strokes of air and light
might have captured his hand;
hereabouts, shift and shunt through
silos of summer heat. The green slope of
hill and high farm road faienced in

gouged lines round the bowl that
holds this town, country-ransomed,
found on a map antique or rumoured.
Buildings ghostly as pieces of pottery
thrown up from a promising dig.

Muffled engines of looters cruise
and idle the outskirts around and round
the bowl of the town, every night,
conspire to crash the bright party as the
sky shatters a million broken stars.

ELECTRICIAN

The electrician lives in a villa of brown clinker brick with aluminium window frames high on a hill in a new subdivision. Smoky tinted glass. The young wife is seen outside on washing days. Daily, she arranges ornate flowers in white ceramic vases behind those windows. A glory of colour that cannot be seen from the outside. She keeps house. From the lounge ceiling hangs one massive crystal chandelier. They live high on the hill with other villas which look the same or that represent variations of sameness. The electrician drives to jobs all over the district six days a week in his van burnished bright with signage.

His wife who knows where he is at any given moment empowers him. She has his lunch prepared daily at 12:30 PM sharp. He stares through the smoky glass windows and says nothing or says very little. Nothing more than is necessary. Why invite indecision? The countryside seen through his windows rolls away in soft brown tones throughout the seasons.

In the middle distance, below on the flatlands, the sewage treatment pond reflects early morning light. Lake Tutae to the locals. One row of poplars, as if scrawled in italic, serve as backdrop. Even at this distance it looks like a man-made lake. Further out still, a little more to the west of where he now sits, a limestone plant, steam pumping from its stack, glows whitely at this early morning hour.

At the bottom of the exclusive, hilly subdivision a short distance into town, the supermarket, barking brand names, bustles with the comings and goings of the townsfolk. The electrician dreams of pylons standing guard over his family and over his domain. They hum to him confidentially. Everything that switches on or off is within his jurisdiction. His sworn duty is to maintain the flow of electricity to every house and family in the district. The chandelier in his lounge burns crystal bright late into the night. Every morning he rides out to meet the call and rescue the town from zombie death.

'tutae' *is the Maori word for excrement*

ANTHROPOLITE MAN

They wore thick leather jerkins. I can't recall the colour, oak brown, or maybe black. The men lumbered like some slow choreographed minstrel show (or mediaeval procession), with giant sacks slung over their backs (bent) round the back of our place to dump the broken load in the cut down packing case that served to house the heaped-up coal. The coal man, sometimes two in single file, stooped, heavy stepped, in foul weather or fine, past our kitchen window. Year in year out they filed by, to feed the wetback coal range, which like some leviathan at home in its bay, occasionally breached, sending a spume of steam hissing and bubbling angrily from the roof overflow pipe, only to subside and exhale with a repeated, regurgitant, gasping. Taciturn, stolid men. I dared not speak to them, but only saw their hunched forms on a migratory track they could not seemingly be deflected from. The Anthropolite Man who lived amongst the seams in a world of gleaming, oily shale, tattooed maybe with fronds and ferns from extinct tropical forests, in spirals that could no longer be deciphered.

THE GREAT REPRESSION

Somehow, we must come up with schemes
to make money in these hard times, move sideways.
Maybe we need a new economic model, like an

installation set in a large space we can all look at.
Hidden speakers would boom, boom with coda,
counting down the steps to capitalistic Armageddon.

This would be such a device as would rival the
water clocks of ancient times—a new wonder!
There would be giant monitors set like deflector

shields from above refracting images of historical
import. Pictures of CEOs dressed in loincloths,
begging. Captain Cook reassembled as John Wayne.

Dusky Maidens seducing five star generals.
The Voice of Doom counting down the days of
the eternal week we dream we are forever trapped in.

T-shirts on sale. Postcards and prints. See the show.
Buy the DVD. 'THE GREAT REPRESSION'
coming to the disintegration of a family near you.

UNDERCOVER

The moon was half. As though the act
of clearing a space in the partially clouded
sky had worn itself away. In the ceiling,
at the eastern corner, above the bathroom,
there under the broken eave, a starling
has made her nest—scraping and pecking
well into the night. I would have preferred a
thrush, well bred and shy, though they
have their quarters happily and secretly
secured in a place I do not know of.
And, ubiquitously, the 'timid temerity' of
the sparrow riotous in a thickly leafed
camellia bush, up against the neighbour's
house, by the dozen, a noisy senate,
the day's activities under discussion, by the
last of the deflected heat off that brick wall.
An Ongarue truck and trailer from the
quarry grinds down the hill past my thickening
barricade of bush and shrub—I get a glimpse,
in part, as it passes along the gaps between.
A Fonterra milk truck and trailer, elongated
and oval, flashes its chrome silver bright,
(white gold flooding the nation's coffers)
and grinds up the hill past my place.
Absent twenty years, I left a country of sheep,
returned to a country of cattle; rivers
wheeze through an iridescent landscape,
gorged on nutrient-rich run off. This is *lower
socio-economic* territory round here in the

North King Country; run-down rentals
and moldering hatreds, hobbled by small
town boredoms. It's pretty, looking out
over the valley at dusk, to the hills, seeing
all the lights of the town laid out brilliant
as LA. But this isn't LA. This is rural New
Zealand, where every woman over forty
looks like Janet Frame in a parallel universe,
of the under privileged. This is a scene
set for the opening of a Western; the danger,
and the standoff; and that is as far as
it gets. As though the locals had lost the script,
or the plot, not sure what move to make
next—if indeed there is ever a next.
The entire rehearsal eddies to nothingness.
But, *what happens* next (and folk will admit to
this), is nothing more nor less than weather.

ANOTHER *Wow! Signal*

How wonderful it would be if we could
truly feel saved from
                        anywhere, out there
that, listening intently, past the Fear-Boundary,
the Unlearned-Lessons Zone, through lesions
of compounded time guided by our
calendar of invention, from concept to
conquest.

                    'Oh night that was my guide'
that on a quiet, uneventful desert hour,
darkening into dawn (no falsehood) you hear it,
on your watch alone, revelation, much like the first time
we heard the whale's transports, truly caught
and recorded; we listened, we heard,
and a belief was born, a hope realized, made memory.

                    And there it was,
regular and regulated, punching its way through
the constellation Sagittarius. Another Wow! Signal.
Until now, a desolation of stars and a hardness
of light. The silence between broken at last on one
narrowband energy spike.

'NO PEN OR PAPER IN PARADISE'

—Nawal El Saadawi

Housed within its crystal grotto the giant plasma
screen creamily uncoils its mantra, one word chasing
languidly upon another, 'Madness is Pandemic'

and, 'In America You Can Get Everything You Want'
over a background of hazed, Maya blue, fathomless.
Chariots of one sort or another crowd the company

car park; Phrygian, Celtic, Illyrian, Thracian; theme park
or anteroom one might have thought, but being dead,
one does not think, for the moment eternally dissolves one

into the other seamlessly; the dream of forever leaning,
the fall, the long look back, the forced look down,
and again, one thought chasing upon the tail of the next.

MILLEFIORI

A drawer sliding on its wooden runners
                suggests a brief, hushed sound, a dryness.
It is 4:30 AM, mist holds the valley,

                rolled lightly, it floats there, a yellow-lit,
ghostly tube. The glass bowl tilts overhead,
                millefiori, galaxies, frequencies, spill.

It is 4:30 AM, at the close of April,
                the smooth rasp of abacus or accordion;
a goods train whose carriages run the

                entire length of this town; closer, the sound
of an abacus—drawing away, that of an
                accordion, exhaling, toward the dawn.

A MIDWINTER NIGHT'S DREAM

It's that time of day when darkness
has clenched the outline of things; the light
is lifted up and thrown away, that last,
tapering, fuse of blueness. Everything appears

at once grounded and in retreat, in one
sense a true marriage, the ritual of heat and cold,
repeated between bouts of escape into other
habits, fearful risk-taking, invasive looks

made back down the days, entanglements,
heartfelt hours, reckonings, set against those
small gains of the selfsame heart; so dusk brings
to book each day and is a graveyard of sorts.

After shifting rain, a cushioning warmth.
The night still. Small rents in the fabric of dark.
Headlights scissoring round a bend, search
elsewhere. Engine hauls heat. Tumblers lock.

GREEN ASTERISK

It is the way out of town, north, over the railway
lines polished by a hundred tyres every hour year upon year,
by rolling stock for longer still, chugging the decades,
clanging the crossings of every small town on the
                Main Trunk Line

where the light runs quicksilver, this way and that,
along the rails. Is this your destination then—why north?
A bigger city warmed by money and all the lust that
want brings, no longer holds the same attractions,
as if it ever did. Necessity has replaced hunger.
One always returns not because it is home, for there is
no other place to go.

                They rise to view, Pirongia Mountain,
Maungatautari, as I pass between them, heading north.
A brand new yellow 4 Square Store lights up main street,
short and wide.

                Bungalows set back amongst
elegant gardens and rough-hewn, stylish stone walls, suggest
that these districts might well be called counties; Waipa,
Waikato, Franklin whose dairy farmers sing the praises of
curds and whey all the way to the bank.

                The wives lack a
city, money gives them privilege, protection, which clears
a space round them, empty ownership of air. A cabbage tree
pins its green asterisk to the ridgeline.

         An hour on this back road loops back,
the pull of State Highway 1, heading north at Ngaruawahia.
The Waikato river running dead silent alongside; road,
rail, and the river seemingly abandoned, its surface
a pummelled pewter.

Behind you the copper tinged, cattle-bowed paddocks.
Blockish silhouettes. Cubist installations propped there under
a question mark of trees.

To the city as particle accelerator.
                    You draw to that magnet under a
passing squall, and those ink blotches across the windscreen
are tree crowns seen through rain.

To that coastal city flat on its circular rim at the end
of this battering-ram highway, embossed as a warrior's shield,
or bright and young as a rubbish tin lid.

TRACKING RUPERT BROOKE

Had he stayed longer, one could easily have imagined Rupert Brooke strolling down the country roads and lanes of the North Island of New Zealand, an Edwardian in an otherwise Victorian South Pacific country, knocking the heads off dandelions with a switch, but given that he stayed a mere two desultory weeks, more by default than anything else, this is not possible. He was, after all, a man in a hurry, and—though perhaps only half-realised at the time—he did have a war to get to. An early, midsummer morning in the country.

Let us assume Rupert's sensibilities were wistfully inclined, directed toward an English rural setting; before him, as if in the mind's eye, he might have seen: '*At seven o'clock the new risen sun, bursting through the oak leaves, made a perfect spider's web of silver rays. Sky and earth were misty. The grass-blades and bramble leaves were dewy grey, the dandelion clocks were all over diamonds, at the edge of the dusty road: the elderberry bunches hung heavy and drenched above them.*'

Just as Edward Thomas had observed such a scene in his essay, 'London Miniatures'. But this was not his England, nor anybody else's. Rupert had bade farewell to his hosts, the Studholmes of Ruanui Station located just out of Taihape, where he had stayed for a few days, and who on his request may have dropped him on the outskirts of this small country town where he was happy enough to walk the mile or so to the Taihape train station (even though his foot, poisoned in Fiji, continued to trouble him a little) to catch the Wellington Express, and there take a boat to Tahiti on his return to England, and then onto his final destination—the imminent, First World War.

The country was troubled by strikes and he considered the women if not ugly certainly dowdy. While waiting for the train he angrily scribbled free form poems about the death of beauty and love's demise. In disgust, he stuffed the crumpled notepaper into a hole in the station waiting room wall. The hole had been made by a violent kick from a working-class boot. These poems would have revolutionized modern poetry. They were never found.

APOCRYPHA

Fog percolates through inaccessible valleys. A mackle-faced moon. Lyricism is a herd of goats that scatters into the bush line. No precipitate ridge-to-ridge leaping here. This is not ancient Greece (the Greece in thrall to its gods), and certainly, not Europe. It is a dream of mediaeval cartographers. This is the southernmost archipelago; a largely temperate climate, and memoried by a handful of glaciers, white wolves retreating into an alpine landscape. No one lives here. There exists moss, forest, dripping fern, and tussock. This is its language, but because no one lives here the language has never been spoken. Even the suburbs stand empty like some failed dream of the unarrived. Houses are a handful of croutons thrown over lumped up hills. As if the Great Confectioner, in one moment of joyous release, flung from his palm little cubes of manna. It is understandably very sad, and much like a journey never taken.

CAMBER SWING

Broken eggshell moon 10 AM the hawk flying out of it
tethered to the ribbon of back country loops angling on road
kill between hill's buckling panels that bury shadow
windscreen flashing light back on the eye of hawk itself

a circling shadow hovering in the rear vision mirror as
that bend falls way behind slung on the road's camber before
and after on hill wave one after another contracting spine
of train and carriage multiplying in a line containers

locomotive drawn 80km/h through tunnel and small town
clickety-clack past cattle-crowded paddocks with sheepfolds
in retreat fairyland and demon land bound clouds gathered late
afternoon west making for a watchable sunset crickets hard

at it in stereo under the sun lavishing amber oil on feta yellow
chunks of limestone strewn about front yards—kerbside.

THE DEPARTED GUEST

His skull is an abandoned amphitheatre,
empty of echoes, the green tinge to the inner
cavity his last twilight dream of ancient forests.

And here, follow the traces of the two weathers
that afflicted his dreams: *hope*: that always
meant the future, and: *fear*: the drone of a past
that could never be undone.

      Over time,
the parietal plates of his skull drifted apart,
the Pangaea of his centre, constructs of his thought,
set out in a system of the rationale, all fell softly
aside, without so much as a whisper.

Decomposition began from the inside out,
unhurriedly, merciless and unstoppable as rumour.
That other, the one within him,
      departed the bastion
of his being, silently, and without his knowledge.

SCARECROW

An ANZAC Day Reveille for Peter Olds

Could any sane man answer your query:
'Put Jesus in the trenches, what would he do?'
In that triumph of the Industrial Revolution
men became ghosts for monuments yet to come.
He might've gone AWOL for all we know,
ask those generals who made a botch up of it.

Agitating in armchairs over port and cigars,
'Did our duty for King and Country,' something
about the Boer War. Jesus at the front line?
Another troublesome 'conchie' could've
been put to better use, slackers not permitted,
crucified for all to see in no man's land.
Jesus strung up—a bedraggled scarecrow;
no barb wire crown of thorns, nothing showy.

Just another broken body, flesh and blood,
tied to a makeshift frame, angled into the mud.

ROAD NOTES

'The traveller is the aggregate of the road'
—Antonio Machado

I
Troopers Rd, Te Kuiti, karst country,
mediaeval ruins and cloud-moats, hills afloat.

II
Dragged-down hills and pocket-cleft bush
over the Waikato River moving with
chain mail sluggishness.

III
Flat bottom clouds. Paperweights.
Slide above the horizon on wires and pulleys
realistic as false scenery.

IV
Rolling stock. Cutlery crash of carriages behind
a blue, yellow-nosed locomotive hauling through Huntly.

V
One sooty white horse standing alone in
a paddock, still as a plaster cast.

VI

One lone container dumped beyond the farm
gate, under the copse, squat as a bandit's bungalow.

VII

Low-flying squadron of magpies.
April hung up to dry bright on shadow rafters;
the first frosts glaze the lawns.

VIII

A convocation of cabbage butterflies
dance out of focus, whitely, across State Highway I.
Over the Bombay Hills.

VIX

Curving paddocks off the Bombay Hills raise
an eyebrow of hedgerows facing toward Auckland.

X

Wolf-grey quarry of greywacke gouged into
hill valley set well back across the river on my left—
a palisade of pine trees lurching at its rim.

XI

Daylight. Interrogation light. The white
burning circle. Locomotive rounds on me briefly.

XII
Lone shunter. (At night).
'Haven't seen one of
them round here for a long time,' said Ziggy.

XIII
Why did the hedgehog cross the road?
It didn't. Squashed pincushion flat. Burger meat.
'Don't see none of them round here no more.'

XIV
Velvet sheen is maize stubble, combed back
in lit rows, as I head north, buzz cut back from sunrise
to sunset. Paddocks either side. Autumn litter.

XV
A portion of this paddock slopes to a pine grove.
Memory has pulled tent pegs and moved on.
A sadness of light is all that remains, the mould broken.

XVI
Anything is possible, he thought, fog
broiling off rounded hills, the black note of the road
fading off into valleys,
         light aquiver, whiteness
pulled apart, letting the blue into the morning.

XVII

The road that held my house, earliest memories,
forever curved away out of childhood.

XVIII

Between the mile-high voices of adults to
unruly mood states I had never known—
that road sculpted by the confines of the day.

XIX

Stop-go, chain gang compression;
southbound goods train, again, running by the river.

XX

Bulk cloaked billow of steam tapered to
one double stack.
      The Huntley Power Station,
its genii released, glowering down upon the long mirror
of the Waikato River. Still as mercury.

XXI

A car reverses out of the driveway,
comfortable crunch of gravel under wheel.

XXII

High beam hauls in the white line;
the Milky Way, its skid mark slung across the sky,
runs out of steam.

XXIII

The Huntly Power Station under drizzle.
Overlord of the river. A mediaeval shadow block.
Dilapidated cottages thrown about its base.

XXIV

Milk-glutted, Fonterra tankers line up at the
Te Awamutu factory gate, chrome-bellied, sleek fat cows.

XXV

State Highway 3. That rotten log fallen
across the saddle on the western hill ridge and ribbed
with golden moss is sunset.

XXVI

Mid-summer. High green staves of poplars,
even when stilled, look wind washed. The *en plein air*
artist who painted them has just left.

XXVII

Limestone pedestals, empty air, this
backcountry road. I think of statues that lined avenues
to the Ancient Agora of Athens.

XXVIII

Passing Lane 400 m ahead—a lake-wide river,
pond still, but deep;
                an island flat as a barge painted green
anchored mid-stream.

XXIX

Tyre screech. Magpie warble. Morepork's
soft call. Town lights come on, slow yellow, hum of
fridge door left open. Dusk.

XXX

Green glow of paddocks
iridescent as a Petri dish. Mezzanine floor of mist
over autumn valleys, roadside.

XXXI

Indeterminate river valley.
Tree stumps and roots piled in a paddock.
Ragged wood smoke in coils,
caught on the plate glass of winter.

SISTER TO THE SPHINX

for Judith Baragwanath

Some poets long ago might have seen you as
odalisque reclining at one of those old Ponsonby
parties. Oh you were far too upright for that.
You who are sister to the sphinx, how is it then,
beautiful women soften the air about them as
they glide in a movement that is all about stillness?
Maybe it is the shock-wave effect. A mystery
to me and to every man—women too, I expect.
Castled on your lonely Isle in the Hauraki Gulf,
should the aged poet finally make safe harbour
past the headland, to anchor in the calmer waters
of your gaze, would you without hesitation,
leaning from the heights of your self-imposed exile,
reach out one porcelain hand to buoy him up?

THIS WAY OUT

In the fossil record is found no remnant
of the body's soft tissues, these things melt
away, substances by which we sense
ourselves; petrified bone and the catacombs
that riddle bone remain. The rest melted
away. What we were awaits to be uplifted
by some mountain range yet to be born.
Pressed as if some marker between sheets of
schist we become geology. Our home a
mountain axis. Prevailing winds the gathered
breath of ourselves and all our dead.
Such thoughts are composed of solitudes.
Startled, we drop back through the trapdoor
of dream in endless S-curves chasing the
far distant notes of Orpheus as he plays
so high and sweet on his moon bone flute.

TITAN LOVE SONG

No more warnings. Biodegradable soul.
                      Values emitting vapours.
The suffusion of your ultraviolet laughter.

The orange glow of your dissolving gaze.
We sat by the sliding tar of snaking methane rivers,
razor sharp ravines and cloying horizons!

                    Such impenetrable haze.
The cloak of our love held us spell bound.
From such dissolution,
                how we craved
terra morphing, the untrue green of our dreams—
transformation to an oxygen-based life form.

Yet vulnerability and need disgusted me.
Our interactive break down of each other's delights;
you are precipitate and I, particulate.
                My ethane embrace, your methane kiss.

Once upon the vast flood plains
of Titan we grazed the hydrocarbon sand dunes
and drank our fill of benzene.
                We met and mixed on that memorable
month of heavy storm clouds and thick,
methane rain drops.

By the dark regions of *Senkyo*, *Aztlan*, *Fensal*,
upon the cryovolcanic dome of Ganesa Macula we
gazed up into the icy rings of Saturn.

Under the brow of the Xanadu mountains,
from *Ontario Lacus* to *Ligeia Mare*,
by those black lakes we pledged our unloving bonds,
sang our mineral ecstasies.

BAKED POTATO

I take a bright kitchen knife, spear the baked potato from the oven, dry parchment rasp and pop, transfer to my dinner plate, then with a serrated little black-handled knife I saw down the middle, the potato steams and rustles. A Sybil's grotto. Gasps its doughy breath. Then I cram in sour cream with a little butter, salt and black pepper grainy as beach sand. A votive offering. Then as I regard this construction, it falls open like a bible, tells tales to my tongue and palate; taste of fields, and memory of farms once measured by the chain; of morning mists rising over the stark and ghostly skeletons of poplars. Wagon wreck by the barn door, the barn with disheveled loft. One barn owl. A scythe blade sharpened on the edge of the moon. Munitions hidden in heavy sacks of barley grain. This cautionary tale from the plosive potato slumped in the middle of my white dinner plate. Still and steaming, fresh as a cowpat on a shiny autumn morning, bleeding in its pool of sour cream with a little butter.

THE TRANSFORMATION

Light decides knuckled contours, capturing loss that catches us all out in the end. We observe this singular moment—such epiphany lead men out into the desert. The soft-pronged leaf of the olive branch found on Classical pottery, the Greeks, then Romans, circled each other for honours with their conflicting and merging gods. Amphorae. Before this articulated stand-off a desert people configured the image as menorah. First light of moon glazed around pottery, under a slow and revolving sky. Silence sheering off into blackness and pricked light. Pressure on the eardrums the hermit knew. Eternal listening. Clay thrown wetly on the potter's wheel. The olive branch, how it lifts up its soft-pronged candelabra against the rain, and then—see how it turns, silvers.

TESTAMENT

Goshawk lands upon the glove with the shock of recognition. We have supplanted the God with ego. After that, it's downhill all the way into invention, great works of art, the ghost of immortality. Sanguine and blinkered attempts to reach past illusion, stave off oblivion. Does anything possess value if we do not bestow value upon it?

O taxonomy of desperation, catalogue of doubt. The imperative that we must not know in order to discover. Humankind's belief system at work. Love, too? The greatest deception of all. The naked self, teetering on the brink of the precipice. Vulnerability meets impending loss.

One man falling off a cliff will clutch at any inaccessible flower in an attempt to stop his fall. That's love for you—grasping at the impossible, hope without foundation. Regret means floating, not falling. Lament also the dismantling of language, lexicon of the poet who falters and fails into obscurantism. That construct wherein ego reigns supreme, declamatory testament to Narcissus, deflected off the burnished shield. Post-structuralists hectoring from Babel's tower drowned in binary codes. In the eye-blink of hawk time accelerates to a still-point at the moment of impact.

LACE

A short blunt street that cuts between two
longer streets back from the riverbank.
The street does not matter. Nothing begins or
ceases here. Nothing matters.

           One house.
A tumble-down brick chimney smokes because
it is winter. An old house fallen into ruin
with the smoking chimney late winter.

A house long fallen into ruin with its grey
plank walls. Planks with gaps between them.
Along the side of this house, as if to contrast
brightness with despair, is set one single,
tall window hung with pure, snow-white curtains.

                  Curtains of fine, filigreed lace,
pure and white and forever new. Behind those snow-
white, lace curtains a young woman in her
bedroom dreams and dreams.

            She dreams of all
that these snow-white curtains promise, behind
a window that is never opened. She dreams,
unseen within her bedroom, through the lace
curtains which fill the room with light that is
fresh and cold as water.

In the ruined house of
grey planks, with gaps between them, under the
broken chimney, the young woman dreams.
She is caught within the glare of her snow white
curtains. They and she become the dream,
this will never stop, it is forever bright.

RENDEZVOUS

I.M. Warren Dibble 1931–2014

You gave me back my words. A reminder.
Your voice I knew immediately. My words gave me
pause, half recalled, how could it be otherwise?

           I heard them in a different register,
as if for the first time, remade. They had all gathered,
those words, in spontaneous,

mass demonstration, shoulder-to-shoulder,
to make a rendezvous. Whether this was expectation or
conclusion, greeting, or decisive farewell,

in a town square, down highway, for one moment,
I could not tell, those words, disowned, independent.

Given back to me within the single minded
character of your voice, tremulous, through the cable
beneath the Tasman Sea.

The phone call reversed its charge and two poems
informed me newly. Then you hung up.
           Nothing more needed saying. A gift.

Warren Dibble died on Sunday afternoon July 27, 2014 in Sydney.

NOCTURNE

All night, the footpads of these ghosts
amongst the walls, harried as waiters between the
mortal, and some unseen command centre.

        Orders taken and given,
the silent traffic of night coming and going …

As though one half of me had not emerged
from the marble block, the live side, perfectly formed,
held there by that dead weight.

        The dream, and the waking.

The mind a sinkhole. Jumbled cinematic frames
forming and reforming. Taut silences.
        Nocturne for the soul's restive tossing.

    And the breath that in dead earnest
wakes the body in those early hours of the false dawn.
        That form lowering to my bedside
whose thought caused the body to kick wide awake.

        There is nothing but grainy silence.
A hissing sound, and the darkened objects of the room
        surrounding me.

    The ghostly thought evaporated.

HOUSE OF OCCLUSION

After reading Tatiana Shcherbina

Left open long enough spiders will weave these
windows shut, then my world would become a web,
as though I were peering back through old age
as if through gauze, not knowing if that glimmer lies
behind or ahead of me. So I consider my imagined
blindness from plan view. Is focus an inward,
or outward speculation on this house of occlusion?
Spider spells it out in web-letters, by a lexicon of
intersections, through hollow-eyed caves of the dead.
'Buried in our lives we are governed by ghosts.'
My windowsills remain a battleground, bits thrown
about, shattered insignia of the housefly abound.
Yellow and crimson grains of sunset make an altar,
as the oblatory spider pays fully the lares et penates.

THE THREE PILLARS

More belonging to the Decadent Tradition,
    than the Romantic one,
poète maudit. Rimbaud, of course, Rimbaud on the run,
    not from himself, but into himself;

you could say that Chesterton was the one who
    ran from Decadence in the
1900s after a personal crisis of some sort, a malfeasance
    not suited to his outlook in the least;

his personal worldview was destined to embrace
    a laughing God, though
I have always felt that such a God was more dangerous
    in the upshot than a vengeful one;

he does, after all, get the last laugh, at least with
    a vengeful God you feel
as though, yes, you will always lose, but terms can be
    negotiated for your capitulation,

your surrender to the victor out of the smoking ruins—
    you, the *arriviste*, who dared
to question; that is how dictators come into existence,
    the discovery that anger is exhilaration

at authority questioned—from there it's straightforward
    ruthlessness, strategy, all the way
to gold braiding and epaulettes, the laurel crown—Caesar
    liked to wear one on public occasions,

to cover up his bald spot; now, there was a
    high achiever—the marriage-bed his war room;
so nothing matters, yet everything matters. In that sense,
    not much has changed; if everything

means nothing—I can live with that, the *poète maudit*,
    arriviste, the Caesar—those
three pillars that support the best of all possible worlds:
    'whose dreams have the forms of clouds.'

RISING GHOSTLY

A Roadside Song for Nicole Sprague

Your statement broke through the surface:
'Know where the drunk-insane boundary lies.'
February, Fairbanks hunched either side
of the frozen Chena River, small cars play it
safe across ice bridges, otherwise, the revving
of snowmobiles, grainy rush of dog sleds.

I see you cut across campus running late to
deliver your tutorial on World Literature—folk
still talk in terms of the interior and frontier
country. I guess your university might be seen
as a trading post of sorts. White mountains
rising ghostly to the north. You drove south,
not telling anyone, to track your interior;
jettisoned hard concerns for others to harvest.

So, you did a runner and left the territory,
and then those 'pesky police' put out an APB.

DARK MATTER

The white moon, a wild mare, driven into the canyon, clouds churned beneath its hooves; toadstools in pine plantations accumulate, some grubby little act performed late at night; green and crinkled, the sheep-terraced hills, white and pink, the purple magnolia bloom.

One singular, brick chimney stack rigid as any branding iron, silent as an exclamation mark. The orbiting, ghost of a house. Beneath and through a copse of native bush, the stream tumbled out of sight, descending into a narrow gorge under the limestone bluff. Looking down from a backcountry road, the whole seen in miniature, suggestive of some pastoral scene not unlike this one. Overall, the sense not of loss but absence.

Once upon a time—but what of it? Nothing happened, no beginnings, endings fizzled out after a few false starts. No discernable joy and even less despair. Nothing happened of any consequence. No fairies at the bottom of the garden, no goblins in the glade.

No agape amongst the livestock; birth and death notices ascended in dizzying columns and as quickly dispersed, like chimney smoke, into nothingness. Dark matter into oblivion. The stream that echoed through the narrow gorge increased and diminished in volume, much as expected, and according to the seasons.

DOMES

A poet was finally selected as the inaugural writer for the W.M. Keck telescope residency in Mauna Kea, Hawaii; one of the world's largest observatories. How was it possible, he asked himself, to write of a universe which, within its vastness, contained no imprint or evidence of human existence? Before him the smoky grey volcanic mountains, the far-off glint of the sea, the dense green of tropical foliage, the sharp mountain air and moon-laden nights. The weeks passed. He wrote nothing.

He felt as insignificant as a bellhop in a palatial but empty hotel. 'My words,' he said, 'belong to an outmoded circuitry.' All about him the calibrated machinery of light-gathering power. The daunting magnitude of Keck's light-bucket. Information became a blur. 'I am as diminished as any one of the million, white dwarfs fibrillating in the heavens,' he cried, 'Anything I might write would be as a spectral signature on the ultra-violet.'

Observatory domes, he finally concluded, were the equivalent of the ancient dolmens, raths and duns contemplating the farthermost quadrants of the Old Universe. To map the cobbled ways of star municipalities, long decayed galaxies through fountainheads of gas. The twelve divisions of the heavens. The five zones of the universe; the torrid, the two temperate, and two frigid zones displayed as digital coda, bronze-white on computer screens. Underneath the soles of his feet, he felt the heavy pull of dark matter, echoes reverberating from when the universe first rang like a bell.

CHORISTERS

Remembered (retrieved) from the Pre-Digital Age as if via virtual wormholes by the loose, chiropractic crack and crunch of spiral carriages shunter-hauled, twisting from one dimension into the next. Thought-by-interlocked-thought, the Word propelled through, transfixed, encrypted onto a stelae of stars, hidden behind the Milky Way. We are the reflection and the mirror, transmission and receptor, observed the cosmologists. The papal bull declared that theologians, ex-officio, as guardians of mythology, relocate to the Elysium Fields. Here, resided the multitudinous and true gods.

Seen from above through wispy cloud, bomb-churned fields stretched and flickered beneath tinfoil light; it was war. Fear eddied in the eyes of soldiers, and one, though not destined to survive, bore witness. Distilled from this the Gospel of Acedia—fragile as any wan flower discovered within the tank tracks of an advancing column. Oral history would, it was determined, fall to the rumour-mongers. Musicologists, guided by a convocation of choristers, reassembled the broken remnants of song, barely audible, locked within the stone.

THE WAITING

After rain, a still evening, the gathering dark,
cloud cover a grey-blue. Quietness. Starter engine
of the morepork. A test-run. Soon, the full-
throated, measured call from high up on the hill,
behind this house, itself an engine room of
sorts, gently reshuffling in its frame, the air cools,
floorboards creak with the footpads of ghosts,
the fridge digestibly, chirrups, and exhales.
The low hum of a car, unseen, passes on through
the night, lengthening along the valley road.
Darkness thickens. The waiting. Deeper quiet.
And still the morepork has not sounded its first,
questioning call at this hour. One dog barks
at some backyard swing standing still as a gibbet.

PHALANXES

I reached the Place of Staples in your book
Juan Cameron   the pages fell back to become
one plain without boundaries or—horizon—

two ranks of words one corralled in Spanish
while the other stood at ease in English
engaged in conversation at the Place of Staples

without boundaries   abandoned entreaties
No defenderé las últimas posiciones
'I will not defend the last positions' fronted up

at the Place of Staples whose airy currents
of accents mingled or rode up over my thumbnail
without so much as a bump   echoes thinned

to silences that trembled briefly above those
words—frozen into phalanxes—facing off forever
upon that wide plain   at the Place of Staples.

STONE URNS

Not the televised, golf course tournaments,
and the tracked, white ball headed toward its blue arc
that lifts soaringly, but those others, equally
manicured yet more heavily planted out in scrub
and ornamental trees, tethered to some small
town or rural community on a looping back road.

For each of them carries the same secret,
these backcountry golf courses—the ghost of
one shining manor house or country mansion with
stone urns above steps leading onto the patio,
low hedges and friendly topiaries under the imposing
parapets, each floor parading opaque windows.

Grand country houses that were never built
or even conceived of to anchor these ornate grounds—
make of them manorial estates. Golf courses
with low sight lines, pegged out with flags on poles,
over close-shaven greens—and hovering behind or
just above, vaporous, in the most filmic

and translucent of shades, greys and whites,
rises the unconstructed, simulacrum of a mansion
with its rows of reflective windows, and somewhere,
within those cavernous rooms, there would
materialize the slippered footfall, delicate fingers,
brushing balustrade—yet less brutal than Duchamp's

'Nude Descending a Staircase', for a breath
of wind through leaves suggests the rustle of silk.
Unperturbed, golfers, figures in the foreground,
as in a landscape painting, who mill about in no hurry
to go anywhere, could be transferred to a street
corner—as if expectation played no part in the game.

AMONGST VINE LEAVES

for Pina Ricciu

She is young, your mother amongst vine leaves—
head thrown back in a gesture of sensual impatience,
for the harvest festival, maybe, her face belonging
to sunlight that falls low over the hill where she stands
amongst the vine leaves on a Sardinian hillside,
close by her village—dreams as clear and bright as

the air which envelops her. She feels she ought to be
elsewhere, amongst laughter and song, and all the
young men of the village circling her in slow dance—
as in a tryst she would make with herself in the
bedroom mirror—the scented breath of night, cool
and secretive, she dreams of her lover who will carry

her away to far-off places of fashion and glitter
promised by American movies, long silvery streets seen
from skyscrapers, New York accents, the sun warm
upon her bare arms, she stands forever in the vineyard
in that black and white photo, leaves autumn dry, ready
to drift and scatter about her feet, at harvest time.

WRITTEN IN THE MARGINS

Every distraction arrives complete, absorbs
our adoration. This is it. Till again, boundaries
blur distances, shuffle like ash. Another ego
burn-off. The orchards of the soul might have
illuminated a monk's dream, his cell sweetened
by the honey of his God. The desert air blown
so dry it crackles, like wind at the entrance to a
cave; open-mouthed, and silent as any cry of
faith. His palms brush one against the other for
loss and for love. He knows that in the dark,
the stars will rage with light, that the margins of
the Psalms will once again be transformed
into marble columns set aglow by his thought.

BROKEN

for Bob Orr

My brother *Deluxe 1350* portable typewriter. You were at your clattering best back in the 70s, as young as I was, clacked through the days and nights, under wintry, black ribbons of cloud that spooled by, over Reynoldstown high above Careys Bay, up Blueskin Road, toward Mount Cargill. You clattered against nor'westerlies and macrocarpa, clumped windbreaks sloping out across the ridgeline, over rock-strewn paddocks.

You travelled with me back to Wellington, then Auckland, and finally, onto Sydney. Now look at you, keys yellow as old teeth, type bars slumped in their basket. A hollow amphitheatre. O Brother! Such shouts and applause arose from your chest's alveolus. Letters stamped upon the page as your carriage rolled those sheets away. The bell that sounded the end of each line!

It could have been a boxing match. You returned by sea but too late. Unceremoniously, I dumped you on the side of the road. Amongst stained mattresses, broken TVs, soiled clothing. Then, unaccountably, I wanted to make amends. I returned an hour later thinking I could salvage something from the past. To mend your broken metal heart. To assuage my sentimental one. Nothing was found. You had been cleared away with the garbage. A fitting end, brother, I thought. We had both moved on, though not without regret.

YELLOW CHEVRONS

An old story. Our hero wakes up disoriented in a strange and unfamiliar land. Rock strewn, treeless. He is amnesiac; expulsion from Eden is false memory. The Ruskinesque, quartz blaze of a fallen rock. Into his field of vision float half-erased memories. The plank-hulled ship stretched upon the leek-green sea, for instance. Though how did he get here? Balloon-cheeked clouds puff powdery gusts from every quarter. The ship tilts toward its destiny, sails pot-belled and proud. An empire in red shading and black lines spell out emptiness. A clutch of minuscule palm trees lean toward the coast. A few towns and oases marked out phonetically in copperplate promise little. Inland remains largely terra incognita, a persistent rumour. He observes a lizard, frozen beneath his shadow, its back patterned with yellow chevrons. This reminds him of ship's anchors. The map fades off, borderless, into obscurity. The horizon swings on its boom in one slow arc either side of the perpendicular. The emissary has not yet returned with news from the ant-headed people. At best, trade routes remain speculative. Twilight is the texture of wickerwork all around him. Soon the stars.

THE VENDORS

It was only upon reflection. The glimpse suggested light welling up from the darkness of the storm water drain had shifted his orientation. All the translucent icicles melted so that what lay before him was indefinable as grey sludge. The monitor into which he gazed, a digital crystal bowl, only gave back to him myriad distractions at any one time. These annulled every question he might have asked had he understood the need for one. As if an answer were necessary to his investigation. But what might this disclose?

Images and banners passed before him in procession over the plains of the monitor like a mediaeval pageant or armies on the move. Then he realised it was nothing more than the marketplace rabble. Vendors selling their wares silently as if in a mime. Only at the farthermost stalls, on the outer circle, could be heard the sound of something abandoned as though an echo had bounced and broken. He knew then agitation as movement had replaced focus. There was little danger—for the crowd would not cohere and no one sought common purpose. As long as he held onto this one notion he knew that retreat into something he had forgotten was possible.

COMB

The razed city with its grids, blocks,
rectangles, edges worn as molars, as if to
say, 'I am archaeology, seek me
out millennia hence; I am no longer a city
in a hurry—I am privation.

                My bronze gates
torn from city walls; all the hubbub
of the market-place you will find here—come
sift through my ashes, you will discover
a brooch celebrating joy and sorrow of one life.
Here you will find some turquoise comb,
that knew the tresses of a high-born lady from
this portico, overlooking an enclosed
garden, her hair red-gold as those helmets
that entered the orchard, and found
her felled there, under the sun's blade.'

STILL LIFE WITH BOULDERS

Oparure Road, Waitomo

Not quite stubble, more the plucked flesh of fowl,
after the maize harvest, cut to the grain, close cropped
paddocks. An April sun draws shadows across the land,

velvety black, thick as sump oil, the air glass bright,
though filtered as if the light voltage had dimmed, but
nothing as definite as that, except for the sliding

partitions that are invisible, so that the plucked flesh
has become crew cut paddock, and barely a minute gone.
The scene slipping by seemingly so ancient every second

caught up in an eternity of stillness, and the light that
lacquers the surface of everything, shiny as an iridescent-
backed beetle on line-after-line of maize stubble,

in the slow, wondrous tilt of the earth, barely audible
yet felt—each valley holds its own set of mediaeval ruins,
as if one fortified town had fallen one after the other,

reduced to foundations of stacked limestone, half buried,
boulders strewn over hillsides, loosed from some
trebuchet; violence long since returned to the underworld.

THE WORLD'S BASEMENT

The secret lies in memory forgotten; to look
forward is to view perception within the mirror,
staring back, shock of journeys taken, buried.
Everything forgotten is what you know,

has been done, continuously, stumbling back
through the mirror, broken, bleeding light.
Night appalls with its slow, dragging weight,
Lethe-wards slide into sleep; crocodile hours.

Once, within a wadi in the Sinai desert, I heard
the echo in the rock—startling against silence,
as if Orpheus played upon his harp soundlessly,
his touch so exquisite you sensed the sound

all around; that he had never ceased singing his
music, filling the world's basement to overflowing.

WHAT ANGELS THROW

Panels of light and shadow I studied as a child
became a sort of kitset built into my future—paths of
sunlight through blocks of dark, foundations to
somewhere not yet reached; a comforting aloneness.
One private act of knowing I was only half aware of,
mood shaded the colour of twilight I trusted, and as I did
so, aloneness turned to lonely, and I knew I was
on my way, headed toward uplands that lay years ahead.
I wondered how to make sense of those patterns,
that portcullis of light and shadow there before the
beginning, small corners of the world where angels dallied
between tasks, taking a break, to toss rings of light
onto lengthening poles of shadow from dawn to dusk.
A game for them that can never end, maps of the world
rolled up from one season's end to the next, endlessly.

BREAKING STRAWS

I.M. Jack Gilbert

Clouds scrawled orange in Arabic across sunset.
In the foreground, a darkened oscillation of pine trees
underpin it. Two short vapour trails momentarily
appear, one after the other, fade on the translucent
blue. Here is the perfect turning, the statement closing
out the day. You look at the stacked-up furniture
of thought, its shoved aside intrusiveness—measure of
moments that made up the abandoned hours.

       Jack Gilbert makes love sound
like loneliness because it is, as the happiness it generates
is too; and because he recalls this repeatedly in the
body of a lover as beauty—scent remembered starkly
as a Greek Island. He understood transparencies.
Sound not quite right, as if someone were breaking straws.
Music bigger than a village, days that amounted to
lifetimes through all the jumbled light, made sense later,
or some other sense. At the time you gave this scant
thought, buoyancy of the moment holding you back.
Birds singing as light freshened and gave way to dawn.

STONE LINTEL

The gift of slowing time belongs exclusively to
beautiful women and the space they inhabit. As if
the world in a half-turn stopped to listen;
silence in the pause that amounts to humming,
the slow rotation of a Greek vase, exquisite
decoration, the dance revealed as distant song.
Her look acknowledged as desire for flight—
flickered in the eyes from that beauty encapsulating
her as she posed there under the stone-lintel,
cameras snapping at her heels like lap-dogs. It is
beauty she can only escape from into images
captured, taken of and from her, there in Annandale;
before the old pile known as The Witch's Hat.

DILAPIDATED DREAM

You come upon Piopio (named after an extinct
bird) by hilly, King Country back roads, as if turning
the page on a wall calendar in a rundown motel.
The town appears staged, and empty. Deus ex machina
pulls cloud bumpily across a sky painted achingly blue.
Toetoe rustles over buckled fences. A Sunday,
lonesome sense pervades. Poplars lean slightly before
a furtive breeze; impressionistic sentinels ranged
twelve in a row, under the hillside shadowfall, seen
from the passenger window, as you make the leisurely
descent into the green amphitheater of the valley
below, only ground level hiss of ennui, stridulating
crickets whittling away the afternoon. The sun turns on
its revolving stage as you exeunt on SH3, roadside
hoardings boast strawberry, raspberry, and blueberry—
take your pick. You spot a marae off to your left
(red ochre painted gables) reminiscent of a Swiss chalet;
mustard-coloured, corrugated iron woolsheds dot
the landscape, a dilapidated dream of sheep farming.
Stage lights dim as Fords and 4WDs light up, switch back
and forth, as though pulled along on invisible wires.
Just then a gondola moon hoists over the black backdrop.

DUENDE

Sound at depth is hunger for stillness, in-drawing
of nothingness, the breath that is non-breath, multiple
and profound. Sounding the void has nothing to
do with stillness. No Hadron Collider can ever capture
particles that grace the nuclei of stillness. None can
be found. Such depth is limitless as the stillness imparted
to it—to that which listens back to your listening.
It is endless and constant, neither question nor answer,
heard yet not heard. This singularity of mind that
predates memory—nameless, immemorial, indifferent—
asks nothing of you in its passing but that you see.

COCKAIGNE

The hydrologists were unanimous—not all rivers flowed to the sea. Many had stalled. River mouths and estuaries silted. The mightiest of them grown sluggard (the river in a coffin) inched in eddies, trending sou'west, opened its palm arthritically to the sea. Transmontane systems yet made a show of it, garbled through gravel, under bridges, pushed coastward. There were no 'rivers great and fine / of oil, milk, honey and wine' as heralded by the wandering scholars who laughed loudly at the afterlife.

The unveiling of The Temple of the Sacred Cow, a cacophony of pump and filter, rose twenty storeys chrome bright, overlooked vast river plains to the north, garlands of pennyroyal heaped at its base. Along the horizon, high risers (fallen angels) glowed incandescent into the night as if they had stolen fire from the heavens. What of those river gods and creatures celebrated in bestiaries? Scouting parties of laboratory technicians took samples from tributary and anabranch; found no indicators for marine life, only ample evidence of emptiness.

THE GREAT ROGATUS

He takes our breath away, does Rogatus the Mexican Funambulist, on his high wire strung across the Rio Grande. How confident he is. How audacious! Each elegant footstep placed one in front of the other, just so. He even manages to wiggle his hips for the girls watching, breathless, either side. Look there, emblazoned across the back of his black velvet tunic, The Great Rogatus. *La Grand Seigneur* of empty air!

He pens love songs in Spanish. 'O my sweet Estrella,' he trills, 'My little cake of soap, you attract me stronger than any fridge magnet,' he croons, stepping lightly, 'but you slip too easily from my grasp.' Then he stops. What a showoff! With a flourish, produces a bouquet of red roses from his white ruffle shirt, sheds petals into the chasm yawning beneath. The river, one meandering, silver thread, shiny as the stitching on his damask slippers.

On he goes stealthy as a police informant. A breath of wind quickens. Not even a lover's gasp can unsettle him now. He will make it, adept as translation into a second language. He dreams that one day, on some small archipelago far, far away he will walk between the Ivory Towers of Academia. He will enrapture everyone. Rogatus the Mexican Funambulist has reached the other side—and not one hair out of place.

SLOW RELEASE

In Manaus, Brazil, the Rubber Barons of the 19th century served champagne to their horses and sent their laundry to Portugal. They imported prostitutes from Europe, and lived a life in imitation of the Belle Époque. Carrara marble, late Renaissance art brought from Italy glowed within these jungle mansions.

The local, rufous-skinned Indians worked the plantations for a pittance, driven on by an habitual and 'sustainable' poverty—a V-cut groined into the bark of the tree (*Hevea brasiliensis*) allowed the milky latex to drip into buckets at such an impossibly slow rate, you wondered how such vast fortunes could ever have been amassed.

Nevertheless, a laticiferous guarantee of dynasties for the colonists and their imperial industries abroad. This was style and exploitation on a grand scale. Columbus who 'discovered' the Americas in 1499, found Brazil eight years later—first the parley and proffered help, then finally betrayal, that mother of invention, inevitably unfolded.

The steady annihilation of tropical forests followed, just as the human body, similarly cut, subsides into death as the blood ebbs from the wrists, and into the tepid bath. The slow release of consciousness; that voyage into darkness, disclosed sacrifice, shamanisticly conjured.

LUXEMBOURG

for Jossy Gerö

Heading toward Luxembourg, I picked up
a truck ride at the Belgium border one afternoon,
arriving at the old city centre around dusk,
late spring, 1979. One building drew me to it.
Tall windows chandelier bright in the gathering dark.
Nearby and unseen, a deep sandstone gorge
bisected the mediaeval fortress city; tree-thick
parklands beneath welled, washed up against sheer
cliff walls—the Adolphe Bridge grandly spanning it.
A quiet quarter of the old city, laneways dimly lit,
the Café and Bar illuminating one small square.
Waiters drifted between tables with an air of studied
indifference. Girls gathered, languidly confident,
elegantly seductive; devotees of the decadent—
or so they saw themselves. I had come to the city on
some false pretext, what I sought did not exist here.
I do not recall if I found lodgings, or whether
I slept on some stranger's floor later that night; I
remember light spilling onto the square, girls' laughter.
Over my shoulder, within the vaulted amphitheater
of Central Europe, her raised, jade-green eyes, gazed
out on the darkness from a balcony in Vienna.

LUXEMBOURG

für Jossy Gerö

Auf dem Weg nach Luxemburg fuhr ich eines Nachmittags
per Anhalter in einem Laster von der belgischen Grenze aus
und kam im Zentrum der Altstadt in der Abenddämmerung an,
im späten Frühjahr 1979. EinGebäude zog mich an. Hohe Fenster,
kronleuchterhell in der beginnenden Dunkelheit. Unweit und ungesehen
halbierte eine tiefe Kluft im Sandstein die mittelalterliche Festungsstadt;
das Baumdickicht von Parks quoll unten, gegen die schroffen Felswände
gespült — die Adolphe-Brücke überspannte sie mit großer Geste.
Ein ruhiges Altstadtviertel, die Gassen trüb erhellt, das Café
beleuchtete einen kleinen Platz. Kellner trieben mit bemühter
Nonchalance zwischen den Tischen einher. Mädchen trafen sich, von
trägem Selbstbewußtsein und verführerischer Eleganz; Jüngerinnen
der Dekadenz — so jedenfalls sahen sie sich selbst.
Ich war unter einem falschen Vorwand in die Stadt gekommen, was ich
suchte, gab es hier nicht. Ich weiß nicht mehr, ob ich ein Zimmer fand
oder später nachts bei einem Fremden auf dem Fußboden schlief;
Ich erinnere mich an das auf den Platz fließende Licht, an Mädchengelächter.
Im gewölbten Amphitheater Mitteleuropas hob sie ihre jadegrünen
Augen und blickte über meine Schulter hinaus
auf die samtene Dunkelheit, von einem Balkon in Wien.

Übersetzung: Heinz L. Kretzenbacher

IN THE BLINK

Drought is the story of absences, equidistant
and everywhere—hills tawny, baked brown as
bread, light-tilted shadows that fall tall as
statues toppled. After the revolution, fields lay
bare, braided in rusted metal, mangled into
sculptures by moonlight. Mostly, the lamentations
had subsided. A moment of calm, but for how
long? Day and night, women picked through
the rubble, backs hooped, bent to the task, head to
toe dressed in black like giant birds of prey,
shuffling amongst broken ordnance, garments
dragging weighty as wings. An image snapped from
a television screen in the blink of an eye, recurrent
as nightmare, the same scene repeated with
machine-gun rapidity; a thing of terrible beauty.

WORRY BEADS

If there were no God I would pray for the things
I have ceased to believe in; I would pray against fear
of losing faith in the things that I do believe in;
there would be no cold nights in the desert, no beads
of perspiration, nor the black beads of the Rosary
held as dried seeds between my fingers to ease pain
—no, Greek worry beads would be my choice,
one simple, straight-backed wicker chair, and a small
marble top table at some taverna in the shady village
square, or harbourside café on an island in the
Cyclades—and there, prayers that are not prayers,
for the things I have lost faith in, or fear losing,
would issue from the mouth's temple up into that
liquid light, formless as breath, and these prayers that
have no name, nor name any god, would simply
celebrate themselves in an act of soundless wonder.

SIGNS

The star that departs from the pack,
horizontal and flashing, regular as a pulse,
indicates you are alone. Echoes visually
impact your cranial cavities. God is Guesswork.
This is as it should be. Heartbeat as puppet-
show, shadow-play. The devil describes
the detail, intaglio figure, razor-winged, cower
—ing over his prey, the victim savoured.

Again, we despair of mediaeval pits.
Gargoyles leap through flying buttresses of
Notre Dame, Meaux, Cologne cathedrals,
into our wonderful, worst dreams—escape is the
past, mystery of the well, its surface stilled
and furnace-black; your face reflected,
become star-puzzle. You bleed unknowingly
into that wavering dark. 4:49 AM you
awake to star fall slash sou'east the horizon.

Open-Learning Workshops / *morning*

Advice to a novelist

Supply the characters of the story with a set of travel-brochures, then let them talk amongst themselves. NB: your characters must always be vastly more intelligent than you are. This immediately puts you above critical notice. Buy a sheep dog and avoid rabid socialites at cocktail parties. A sober, disgruntled approach to the reading public is advisable. Short bursts of articulate invective highly recommended. Take up darts.

Advice to a poet

Don't take the whole business too seriously. Adopt long-distance walking as a hobby. Don't become a typographical cowboy or you will be mistaken for a signwriter. Guard against becoming a funambulist sans balancing pole. Failure means you are one step away from becoming a successful copywriter. Success means you are one step closer to never having to write another lousy word.

Advice to a playwright

Invite all those detestable people in your circle to first night. After the show abruptly leave *alone* by taxi for the nearest nightclub. This will prepare you for the morning review notices. Structure your dialogue as you would a scaffold: vocal pictographs around an imagined community of individuals. Discard long monologues about the world gone to hell. All people want to do is get home safely. The more *avant-garde* your play the better; audiences love nostalgia. Acts are for the apostles.

Advice to a landscape painter

Ignore the existing mytho/historical landscape which you have either inherited, or migrated to. You are Adam. Nothing can be created without the imposition of your unique will. Size is important and affirms to the viewer's eye that you are a monumentalist in breadth and neo-classicist in scope. They fail to see that you are a dedicated billboard artist. One day you will move to Las Vegas.

Advice to a linguist

Language? Hardly. Hair-bound words slavering at the mouth's cave. Speech clubbed to falsehood. Why is this so? Listen to production's moist purr which blocks the way back. To where? No sacred groves remain to ask in. Get a job as a taxi driver in a developing country. Storerooms are regarded as primordial, sacred places.

Advice to an English lecturer

Your future lies in the private sector. Stage dinner parties for book reviewers. Court publishers as your *intermediate* friends. Start up a literary magazine with an East European bias and nominate yourself as a cultural commissar. This is your birthright. Push post-structuralist theory through other writers. *Culture = Power = Exclusivity*. You are a cultural supremacist whose root cause is self-loathing in the knowledge you lack originality. Join the local Press Club.

Open-Learning Workshops / *afternoon*

Advice to a philologist

Converse with tramps. Record the patois of those who prefer to live under viaducts as opposed to living in stormwater drains. For a location guide consult your local government sponsored unemployment centre. Avoid detention camps. The language of the tin cup tapped out on bars in high security prisons is central to your understanding and visualising primitive speech patterns. Read George Borrow's *Lavengro*. Move into a housing estate.

Advice to a medievalist

Lecture Notes: Catholic church as living reliquary of medievalism. Opulence continues to flagrantly contradict each new interpretation of modernism and contemporary thought. Catholic authority prevails as anachronism. The last stand of medieval land baron mentality in a virtual world. The monastic spirit is long dead. Universities have sworn fealty to the corporates. Become an itinerant scholar *qua* goliard.

Advice to web designer

You are the modern equivalent of the sandwich board man and the world is your pavement. You carry with you shop frontages of all the cities of the world. When you advertise, 'Eat at Joe's' you create a global franchise. Each page you design is a card plucked from fortune's pack. Your credo: *Everything and nothing has value, the world is a pixelated glass ball.*

Advice to a biographer

You job is to compress time so that personal incident in the life you are reporting on becomes an historical event. This permits you to make logically 'imagined' links in the disordered chronology that is an individual's life. Elevate a life to the level of the subject's recorded achievements. You must disguise the fact that you are merely an officially sanctioned gossip. Your quandary is that *fact* gets in the way of *opinion*.

Advice to a language poet

You have recurrent dreams of a ticker tape parade on Wall Street. You are showered by your own *compositions*. Millions of letters and symbols. This dream symbolises your endless capacity to promulgate disinformation and untruth. The greater the abstraction the greater your success. Obscurantism equals originality which is, nevertheless, a borrowed concept. You are a social media terrorist and disciple of SoundCloud, Instagram, or whatever comes next. Infinity is a manageable excursus.

Advice to a book review editor

One day you will be taken seriously. Meantime, you remain the stooge of book barn syndicates. What author you promote will decide guest appearances at literary festivals, Hyatt Hotel book launches, etc. Safety lies in numbers. Affect an intellectual stance in the manner of a hipster, film critic to secure regular, weekly spots on RNZ and Sunday morning TV talk shows. Join a gun club. Aim one day to become 'reviewer in residence' at a leading American creative writing school.

Open-Learning Workshops / *evening*

Advice to a literary festival director

You are, in essence, the grand puppeteer, politician of the highest bureaucratic order. You must be seen as the non-partisan dispenser of the public purse. Knights Templar of popular, *belles-lettres*. Spend your days and nights in the off season shifting through flowcharts and sales figures from multinational publishing companies in order to make a selection of authors. Beware the *margin call*.

Advice to a literary agent

Your job is to find a publisher for anything that can be written down and sold. Creativity and originality are the least of your concerns. Publishing is a whorehouse, you are the pimp, your clients the pampered customers. You belong to an elite guard promulgating unbridled consumerism and conspire with multinational publishing houses to lock up the market under the motto: *Whoever Sells Wins*. Treat every Ms as a potential film script. Your success like every agent lies in bulk billing.

Advice to a poetry society

You manage a glorified canteen for itinerant writers and a *trash & treasure* market for informal reading venues. As an amateur organisation that aspires to the trappings of the prestigious literary luncheon you are, at your most ambitious, nothing more than an imploding committee in search of a mediator. Your salvation lies in bus tours, to and from retirement villages, and as a sideline, promoting *Poets in Parks*.

Advice to an in-house editor

Grammar is not an issue. Avoid alphabetical lists of first lines and titles as end pages at all costs. In effect, you are a page collator with aspirations toward a doctorate in English Literature and a career based upon your first novel, which remains unwritten. Your job is to look, listen and learn. If you work for a low-ranked academic press, pander to your publisher, who is basically an unqualified sub-editor with no, or little understanding of original poetics, beyond the current, clichéd fashion. Study Kindle and ebook returns. Do not publicly cultivate the company of writers. *Vote Labour*.

Advice to geneticist

Change your hairstyle to traditional fifties short back 'n' sides, or military buzz cut. Avoid corduroy and similar fustian wear in favour of ersatz loafers and chinos. Join a mock combat group for weekend macho bonding sessions in the bush. Write a long narrative sonnet sequence on neural transmitters, titled *Blameless Memories*. Quote J.B.S. Haldane and Professor A.N. Whitehead at every opportunity. Read David Lodge for relaxation during long international flights. Subscribe to the *Icelandic Genome Quarterly*. Write a paper on The Inherited Semiotic Characteristics of the Y chromosome. Secure annual invitations to Icelandic seminars as speaker on a yearly basis. Stand as Independent for your community.

Advice to a young poet

Every thought is an act of translation; translation is the act of sympathetic betrayal. Poetry is the embodiment of memory and truthful record pays homage to it. The literary critic is the foreign agent in the camp. His job is to encode untruth and misinformation. He boasts theoretical abstraction and passes it off as informed judgement. He is in league with the fashionable clique of the day. Know this, and secure faith in your own poetic instincts—if for no other reason than to capture one elusive, revelatory moment.

KITCHEN TABLE

*'Kitchen tables—where would us poets
be without them?'*
           —Peter Olds

The question now arises, how to make a poem
at a kitchen table? Only a small space is required
between the clutter of the last meal and the HP bottle
of sauce bullying the mustard pot next to it.
Should the palette feel jaded, a pinch of angst
and emptiness is recommended. Broken love affairs
are an excellent ingredient, as binding as broken
eggs. To this, add four drunken nights, and possibly an
argument with an estranged partner over not
too much in particular—a desiccated sprinkling
of laughter is optional to add a piquant flavor to the
mix. Beat in one old flame with one tablespoon
of hard luck and low expectations; as to additional
emotional sweeteners, half one disastrous gaff
with a potential partner, and stir well. Let the mix
rest for a while (for some it is a lifetime) then
spoon contents into one baking dish. Set the Oven of
Retribution at 180 °C and bake for 40 minutes—
prod with skewer to check for moisture levels.
Stand for about 10 minutes and garnish with the milk
of human kindness. Serves all who sit and wait.

AT THE TURN

We wrote words with pages in mind.
Each turn a pause made to grasp the visible
in all that went before, suspecting what

came after, echoed back in hoof-beats.
Sound receding into the future as,
unsuspecting, we waited upon our arrival—

uncertainty, not yet coagulate of all
our instincts, turned question. One breath
falling upon the next as ambush, each idea

formed, or half-formed, stood sentinel.
The utter, complete *nothing* gathered to
to silence as if, eavesdropped on, we fled that

footfall before we heard, at the turn,
our body on its pivot, torque to greet the
invisible companion, darkening there.

THE LOST GERMAN GIRL

Berlin is desolate as a ruined beehive,
rows of hollow cells, avenues of piled rubble.
The slow exodus of refugees pulling small
carts a child might own, handfuls of scavenged
items. Where are they going, and in which
direction are they headed? Streets that are the
imprint of streets, spaces that once were
town squares, eddies of dust where fountains
played. Women in straggling lines pass
from hand to hand broken bits of belongings
retrieved from the rubble.

               The lost German girl
listlessly walks a country road near the Czech
border. She wears rough breaches with
loose hanging braces, a black woollen top.
Her face, still beautiful, is bruised.
She puts a hand to her brow and hangs her
head in this short film footage—passes
out of sight forever to an unnamed destination.
The country road and green fields emptied
now.

In the mouth of May another girl sits by
a broken wall in Berlin, stockinged legs drawn up,
her head resting upon her knees, and hair
fallen, too, like a shield, as if to protect.
Into what bright year will these two disappear?

One about to leave Berlin, a ruined dream
and dead nightmare, and the lost German girl,
expelled from Prague. They both exist
between these two purgatorial states, in that
No Man's Land, caught between loss
and despair, in the month of May, 1945.

DISSENTIENT

1.

   Three sparrows, moving toward
the same branch, on the same tree, create an
arrowhead. This is the discovery of
the projectile through avian flight; each
revelation has its value—this going back,
anonymously. Each city has its gravitational
pull (it's where you come from) rural
is always in the remembering; within the
present, slung back behind. You count them
along the backcountry road—twelve
poplars lining some rough driveway up to an
unseen farmstead. I mark them out as the twelve
apostles; a chorus of green candles in
spring that shed yellow through autumn.

2.

   Wind mercurial as Mary Magdalene
disturbs the combed-out soil of one ploughed
paddock. Limestone cave become grotto.
Mary had fled to Provence, gnostic
embodiment of wisdom, divine and fallible.
Cult and myth precipitated ritual, revered
earth as Holy Grail; deepened to sense of place,
light-glazed landscape—rich as mosaic,
broken or brown as pottery placed at
the cave's mouth. Herakleitos said, 'The sun is
one foot wide,' that all the stars couldn't
dispel the night without the sun, that lightning
is everything, that consciousness has no
boundary, is fathomless in every direction.
Air must have appeared as crystalline to him.

3.

   The whole weight of tradition in
shoulder and bicep behind his spadework.
Short, hard thrusts into the backfill,
broken bits of glass and brick, loamy deeper.
'Let me do that boss,' he said. Two
potted pohutukawas transplanted to the
front courtyard of the unit block in Enmore.
The beauty of the practical, his father,
and his father's father knew before him,
back to the olive groves. A Greek
yardman. 'There is no stick hard enough to
drive me away from a man from whom I
can learn something,' said Diogenes,
who knew of this man's brutal elegance.

4.

   Brain-shaped Antarctica. Now stick
a flag up at the South Pole for what you take as
dead centre. Let the huskies hyperventilate.
You come from another life, from the
back-streets and back-stairs of an earlier era.
In this ice sheeted world life is a precious gem.
But at this precise moment your mind
is whiteout—thought a snow blizzard at sea.
From that flagpole of an indeterminate
life you rapidly recede vertically—observe,
sketched across your inner eye, that the
shape of Antarctica resembles a battered bicycle
wheel, whose buckled spokes all lead back
to where you are now standing, oblivious.

5.
   Driest air carries the echo further.
Light and distance over desert silence make
faith possible through *hesychia*. In the
anchorite's cell each sheet of parchment turned,
is a hurdle leap toward the God through
the incantation of scripture as chant.
For him, creation is fear in the guise of hope,
and the vast, underlying principle of
existence has nothing to do with creation.
Existence is, and death exists to humble us.
At Mt. Colzim, rising in the open desert
off the South Qalala Plateau, 20 miles west of
the Red Sea, Saint Antony tends his garden,
and berates the wild asses for ravaging it.

6.
   Flocks of asteroids sweep under
an eternal twilight, multiple horizons by the
spirit level of stars, amassed to galaxies—
formulae; framed there at the cave's entrance.
The desert that fanned out beneath him,
flat as a blackboard, moon swept. 'Beauty can
only exist within the realms of human
habitation, alone,' he surmised, 'darkness
becomes an afterthought. Meaning then is as
much as we might imagine it to be.'
Come morning, he would take up the pickaxe,
again climb the rock face behind him,
and hew one more step up into the mountain
in his journey towards forgetfulness,
each chip of the rock bright as birdsong.

7.
    Rivers are reflections that pass
under mirrors of the curved, black night,
still and cold. Silence—is a hymn to silence,
spilled from the phylactery of the rounded
sky, stars out across the desert floor,
off the mountain ridge, bulking up behind,
rich coinage of the night, but this is
not Mt. Pispir. Air so pure, it is tasteless,
and the sweetest air of all. He breathes
deeply, exhalation is the anima of
this desert place, he the locus of prayer
within it, his faith refuge and shelter against
demons who visit only occasionally now,
rising as wraiths off the rocks at midnight.

STREETS OF KIEV

after Osip Mandelstam

In Red Square, giant plasma screens loom blank
and wall-eyed, there's no news today. The Kremlin

thug needs time to think. He never counts his
losses, pays no heed to them. His mongoloid eyes

turn unperturbedly to the southwest. Any day now,
he will perform the prisyadka in Khreshchatyk Street.

Under the black-belt moon, he cocks one leg,
a kick to the solar plexus, to the groin, to the temple.

Pectorals flex, abs ripple. His favourite cocktail,
Polonium-210, he serves up to those who dare oppose.

His expression resembles that of a firing squad,
this former KGB analyst calculates the odds quiet

as frost at midnight, his every move accounted for:
pieces of tibia, femur, cranium, each precious object

finds a place on his chessboard. Any day now,
he will perform the prisyadka in Andreevsky Spusk.

Prisyadka: *the squat-and-kick move that belongs
to the Ukrainian 'Cossack Dance' known as* Kazatsky.

BUILDING CODE

Digging foundations with Nicholas Reid

Your remark in passing led me into it:
'I spend my afternoons in the crawl space.'
You refer to your mother's house, in Canberra,
digging new foundations. Similarly, my job
is to repair apparently stable structures,
first built according to binary specifications.

These belong to fashionable, linguistically
leafy suburbs of the post-structuralist;
all flashy façades, questionable architectonics,
designs lacking in simplicity. A confusion
of angles and perspectives. I adhere strictly to
the building code, correcting leaning walls,
sunken joists, sloping floors. It's steady labour;
one foot soldier in the service of language.

Breathless, absolutely still, dagger drawn,
I lie in the belly of the wooden horse at dawn.

SILENT AS A LANTERN

Flame is cupola. See it erupt from
shock-blown window frames of tall buildings.

    Boisterous as applause
exploding from theatre galleries. Observe flame's
upward curve, elegant as the carved prows
of Portuguese caravels.

    Blackened, rectangular
buildings, hollowing before uplifted crests of flame.

Imprisoned within this vortex,
colour bends to whitened heat—oxygen sucked
from the bellicose furnace.

    Flame over distance is voyage, prophecy.
Death throes of military campaigns;
otherwise, and always near, armies command it.

When campfires died, they marched, and flame
gripped cathedrals by the throat in a wreckage of light.

Sails dissolved into cloudbank, the false sunset
of cannon fire flickered, went out, silent as a lantern.

Whole cities became ash for archaeologists.

•

Flame is siren. Gérard de Nerval,
strolling the Palais-Royal Gardens, his pet lobster tied
with a pale blue ribbon.

Gargoyles danced prettily on the ramparts
of Notre Dame for him.

One of the poets known as *les bousingos* who came
           together in riotous company over
potent rum punches, and ice-creams served in skulls—

Théophile Dondey, who 'wore glasses in his sleep
           so that he might see his dreams'.

Borel, 'with his feline teeth,
melancholy eyes fixed on the spaniel at his feet'.
           lilac scented beard, the mouth, an exotic flower.

On one black and white night, Gérard de Nerval
           hanged himself in the Rue de la Vieille-Lanterne
from a sewer grating with an old apron cord;

he saw it as the Queen of Sheba's thigh garter—
a few scribbled notes on *Aurélia* found in his pocket.

He sought the 'eternal feminine' in the Lebanon,
Istanbul and Cairo, fled the black sun of melancholia.

           'At times he lived gaily as starlings.'

IMPRESS

'and always that special slouch
as if leaning toward another, better, planet,'
      Refugees—Adam Zagajewski

They speak in the language of a landscape
that has vanished, before them and behind them.
They know the words carry an unfamiliar
echo in this land though, insistently, the song
stays familiar, much in the way some valued thing
lost will always remain familiar, the guarded
ruin of memory, familial; the sand drifts that buried
the village, the orchard auctioned off to investors
and chopped down; those remnants held over
from the olive press of sunsets still entraps them.
But this is the new land, and they must forget
in order to rebuild, to believe once again, even
if remembering is only the impress of fingertips on
a clay tablet. What is it then makes us distrust
the laughter in the voice? Big or small, recollection
is an ornamental dagger encrusted with precious
stones placed on display, always within view,
though never within reach, a ritual object laid out
in its glass cabinet, ghostly, yet intensely still.

BLACK SWANS

I.M. Ben Webb

Black swans at Aramoana. The harbour lettuce-green as in a watercolour. Otago Peninsula narrowing off Harington Point, and then the open sea. The stately black swans, the running tide. The Spit. A few run-down cribs, mostly unoccupied, set back amongst a scattering of pine trees, marram grass and driftwood. Its arm curving out as if to protect itself against the dune-forming tides. Early evening in half-light; and suddenly, filling the lounge window at the *Pilot's Cottage*—bridge and funnel sliding past, massive, in slow motion. The stage machinery turning, dead silent, as though in a waking dream. Perhaps he saw this too, in his last moments, alone in that cottage at The Spit. Focused upon the container ship as it slipped noiselessly out to sea, past Taiaroa Head. What was it then, threw back the image of the terrified child from the dark well? Self-loathing made real in that final act. Afterwards, out there in the darkness, riding upon the waters, black swans arched long velvety necks, and turned toward the dim-lit window with its silhouette, framed there.

JACOB'S LADDER

That it took ten years. The Rosetta spacecraft had finally reached its destination. The European Space Agency (ESA) for whom time is an imperative, initiated a few tricky manoeuvres. Time in space is relative. Rosetta and the comet are now locked in a synchronized dance, one around the other. At its closest point the craft will come to within 50 km, contingent on speed and gravity distortion.

High resolution images reveal a duck-shaped tumbling object, about four kilometres long. Its surface, the texture of an ice cream cake, averages temperatures of 70°C. Dark and dusty not (as anticipated) icy and dry.

The Philae lander will be deployed once a suitable target site is located, fix itself to the surface, then drill, sample, analyse. The comet swings in a vast, elliptical orbit between Jupiter and Mars, rushing toward the inner solar system at 55,000 kilometres per hour.

Is there nothing faster than light? Thought is. The comet will tell us what we already know—that the origin of the atomic scale is Jacob's Ladder reaching up into the heavens. Time in space is relative. We listen to an endless oscillation of sound, through immeasurable silences. We seek irrefutable evidence that the human species passed this way light years before.

THE JOURNEY

for Nicole Sprague

Decades of steady writing, unacknowledged, did not trouble him. A craftsman. He lived an ordinary life in order to keep his extraordinary mind intact. The family grown and gone. Forty years a merchant on Brooklyn Heights. The business his father started. Sold every variety of antique clock, wall and column, black mantel and kitchen clocks.

Here, time whispered in hushed tones. His wife dead these past five years. An aloneness that announced an end to things. After all this time he finally completed one book of small lyrics.

He locked up his brownstone apartment. With a trunk full of newly printed books, poems that explored the minutiae of light and shadow over clock faces, those small mirrors of divination, he set out by Amtrak to crisscross every State in the Union. For as long as it took to empty the trunk of books.

Sought out libraries in cities and country places—journeyed across open prairies and mountains to find them. Peaceful work done at a leisurely pace. With a knapsack full of books he entered each library and, casually, walked by check out. No one paid him any attention.

An old man with cloth cap and knapsack. Found the poetry section, slid onto the shelf one copy of his book, correctly placed in alphabetical order, then left as quietly and purposefully as he came. All across America. Then he went back to the brownstone, unacknowledged, and died.

STILL BREATHING

I.M. Derick Burleson, d. December 29, 2016

You have entered into the silences,
become the Alaskan wilderness you so
loved, your death in December
amongst the stark aspen, weighted with
snow—your dreams accompanying
you into those woodlands, Oklahoman,
hunter and fisherman, poet.
And though you continued to lose
weight, your robust frame thinning, in
your email a month before you died, said,
'Fun to be out in the woods hunting
grouse with Mirabel,' beloved daughter,
and with Ziggy the yearling pup.
But then you wasted. 'I have sickened
again,' you stated. Doctors in
Fairbanks could not figure out what the
problem was, had given you every
test under the wintry sun; an undiagnosed
illness had your scent, pursued, hunted
you down, woodsman. In the
emergency ward you weighed in at 61kg.
'I am a skinny boy,' you mock-boasted.
You tracked yourself into the deeper
silences of that unmapped illness, had
hoped to fly to Seattle to find a
diagnoses, maybe a cure. But then you
sickened into stillness, beyond the
yellow pine by the river, 'where red-tailed

hawks snatch those diamond backs
and teach them to fly. Where ospreys
snatch rainbow trout and teach them to fly.'
In your last, wilful email to me you said,
'We have to both survive as one
of my goals is to come visit you while we
are still breathing air.' And you did.

A NOTE ABOUT THE AUTHOR

Stephen Oliver—Australasian poet and author of nineteen volumes of poetry. Travelled extensively. Signed on with the radio ship *The Voice of Peace 1540 kHz* broadcasting in the Mediterranean out of Jaffa, Israel in the late 70s. Lived in Australia for 20 years. Currently living in NZ. He has published widely in international literary journals. Regular contributor of creative nonfiction and poems to *Antipodes: A Global Journal of Australian / New Zealand Literature*. Poems translated into German, Spanish, Chinese, and Russian. Represented most recently in: *Writing To The Wire Anthology*, edited by Dan Disney and Kit Kelen, University of Western Australia Publishing, 2016; *Manifesto: An Anthology of 101 Political Poems*, edited by Emma Neale and Philip Temple, OUP, 2017.

www.ingramcontent.com/pod-product-compliance
Lightning Source LLC
Chambersburg PA
CBHW031425290426
44110CB00011B/532